Bold BOARDS

Ideas & Recipes for Easy Entertaining

ISBN-13: 978-1-56383-607-7
Item #7156

Printed in the USA
<u>Distributed By:</u>

PO Box 850
Waverly, IA 50677

www.cqbookstore.com

gifts@cqbookstore.com

 CQ Products

 CQ Products

 @cqproducts

 @cqproducts

Boards galore

The beauty of a board is that it doesn't have to be difficult or time-consuming to put together; all it takes are some great ingredients and a little imagination. Each board and recipe is meant to inspire, so don't be afraid to create your own variations based on your preferences and what's available to you. After all, it's your board, so build it how you like it.

Board Basics

It's easy to get overwhelmed by all the "rules" out there on how to build the perfect board, but it all boils down to three factors. Take these into consideration and your board will be destined for deliciousness!

Flavor

Cater to palates of all kinds by including a variety of flavors ranging from sweet to salty. Try to find a good balance between light and rich flavors. This allows everyone to build their own pairings and bites.

Texture

The texture of food has a lot to do with both the flavor and overall eating experience. The best boards use contrasting textures to play off of each other. Crispy and creamy, crunchy and smooth, and so on.

Aesthetics

A nice presentation leads to an enjoyable eating experience. This doesn't mean every board has to be a work of art, but a thoughtful arrangement and a pop of color go a long way when it comes to creating a good-looking board.

Elements of a Board

Cheeses Variety is the key to a delicious cheese board. Include variety in the type of milk, strength of flavor, softness or firmness of texture, and style of cheese. Branch out and try cheeses you've never tried before. The most important thing is to include cheeses you like to eat.

Charcuterie Here you'll want to follow the same logic as the cheese. Variety in terms of texture, style, and type of meat will lead to a delicious board. Include an assortment of mild, medium and bold flavors. As always, include what you like and what's available in your area.

Bread & Crackers These are the vehicle on which to build the perfect bite. Crackers are a common choice, but fresh bread, toasted bread, and pretzels also make great options.

Accompaniments This is where the board gets its personality. Fruits like grapes or apples are commonly used to add a touch of sweetness and brighten up the board. Nuts bring some protein and crunch. Pickled items like sweet gherkins, baby dills, or olives have acidic and briny flavors that balance out the rich flavors of the meats and cheeses.

Condiments & Dips Jams, preserves, and chutneys bring a pop of color and sweetness to a board. Mustards add acidity and spice. While these are classic standbys, you don't have to stop there. Get creative with flavors by adding salsa, hummus, veggie dip, or anything else that comes to mind!

Garnishes A little garnish will go a long way in adding flair to your board. Fresh herbs like rosemary, mint, sage, basil, parsley, or thyme make great additions.

Serving Tips

Portions A good guideline is to assume that each guest will eat about 2 ounces of meat. However, if the board is the main food being offered, you may want to double that amount. The same rule applies to the amount of cheese to provide. Be sure to provide plenty of bread, crackers, and accompaniments to make sure everyone gets their fill.

Make it Easy While boards are beautiful, they also need to be easy to eat. Make sure to provide all the essential serving utensils so guests can easily enjoy the board. Spoons for jams, knives for cheese, forks for olives, and so on.

Label it Up Labels are a great way to let people know what they're slicing into. Especially if you've provided a few items that are a little out of the ordinary.

HOW to BUILD
your board

While assembling a board isn't an exact science, it is helpful to have a process. It's best to start by placing the larger items and finish by nestling in the smaller items. This makes it easy to fill in any gaps left on the board.

① Build a Foundation

Start by placing any bowls you'll need on the board. Fill small bowls with pickled items, mustards, jams, or dips and arrange them on the board. This saves you from trying to squeeze them on the board later. It also helps provide a foundation from which to build the rest of your board.

② Cheeses & Meats

Space the cheeses evenly around the board. While it's not necessary to slice all of the cheese, it can be helpful to cut a few slices to give guests a starting point.

Now add any meat (or charcuterie) to the board. Get creative with different ways of folding, piling, and slicing meats.

③ Crackers & Bread

Add a few stacks and piles of crackers throughout the board. Don't worry about lining them up perfectly; randomness just adds to the rustic charm of the board. If you have larger slices of bread, add a small bread basket or cutting board adjacent to the main board.

④ Add the Accompaniments

Nestle in the extras. Fill in any remaining gaps with nuts, dried fruit, veggies, pickles, fresh fruit, herbs, and whatever else you'd like. It's alright if things on the board touch – you're going for a full, abundant look here. Plus, the foods are meant to be paired together anyway, so you'll just be one step ahead.

Have fun with it! Don't fret over placing everything perfectly on the board. It all has a tendency to fall into place when it's all said and done.

LITTLE ITALY

Cheeses: Marinated Mozzarella Pearls *(recipe below)*, aged Asiago, provolone

Charcuterie: mortadella, capicola, soppressata salami

Bread & Crackers: focaccia crackers, sliced baguette

Accompaniments: Castelvetrano olives, pistachios, green grapes, grape tomatoes

Condiments & Dips: fig jam

Garnish: basil

1. Put the Marinated Mozzarella Pearls, Castelvetrano olives, and fig jam in small bowls and place them on the board.

2. Arrange the aged Asiago, provolone, mortadella, capicola, and soppressata salami on the board.

3. Nestle in a few stacks of focaccia crackers and baguette slices.

4. Fill in any remaining gaps on the board with pistachios, green grapes, and grape tomatoes.

5. Garnish with fresh basil and serve.

 *For a unique presentation, buy a thick slice of mortadella and cube it at home.*

MARINATED MOZZARELLA PEARLS

*Mix together ¾ C. **olive oil**, 2 **cloves minced garlic**, 2 T. finely chopped **fresh basil**, 1 T. dried **oregano**, ½ tsp. **crushed red pepper**, ¼ tsp. **salt**, and ¼ tsp. **black pepper**. Add 1 (8 oz.) pkg. **mozzarella pearls** and stir to coat. Let marinate for at least an hour. The longer they marinate, the stronger the flavor will be. Refrigerate in an airtight container for up to 5 days. **Makes about 40 pearls**

Marinated Mozzarella Pearls

Chili Olive Oil

SPICE IT UP

Cheese: ghost pepper Monterey Jack, chipotle queso fresco, honey goat cheese

Charcuterie: peppered salami, cured chorizo

Bread & Crackers: crackers, sliced baguette

Accompaniments: jalapeño-stuffed olives, cherry peppers, green grapes, Bacon & Pepper Almond Brittle *(recipe pg. 23)*, dried apricots, pistachios

Condiments & Dips: Chili Olive Oil *(recipe below)*

Garnish: parsley

1. Put the jalapeño-stuffed olives, cherry peppers, and Chili Olive Oil in small bowls and place them on the board.

2. Arrange the ghost pepper Monterey Jack, chipotle queso fresco, honey goat cheese, peppered salami, and chorizo on the board.

3. Nestle in a few stacks of crackers and baguette slices.

4. Fill in any remaining gaps on the board with green grapes, Bacon & Pepper Almond Brittle, dried apricots, and pistachios.

5. Garnish with fresh parsley and serve.

CHILI OLIVE OIL

*Combine 3 T. **crushed red pepper** and ½ tsp. **minced garlic** in a bowl or jar. In a small saucepan, heat 1¼ C. **olive oil** over low heat for 5 minutes. Remove the pan from the heat and carefully pour the oil over the red pepper mixture, making sure the oil completely covers the mixture. Set the oil aside to cool for at least an hour. Depending on your preference, you can either strain out the red pepper or leave it in for added flavor. Store the oil in an airtight container at room temperature for up to 1 month. **Makes 1¼ cups**

French
CLASSICS *Board*

Cheeses: Camembert, Roquefort blue cheese

Charcuterie: jambon de Paris

Bread & Crackers: sliced baguette

Accompaniments: cornichons, hazelnuts, golden raisins, dried apricots, Raspberry Brie Crescents *(recipe below)*

Condiments & Dips: Dijon mustard, honey

Garnish: thyme

1. Put the cornichons, Dijon mustard, and honey in small bowls and place them on the board.

2. Arrange the Camembert, Roquefort blue cheese, and jambon de Paris on the board.

3. Nestle in a few baguette slices.

4. Fill in any remaining gaps on the board with hazelnuts, golden raisins, dried apricots, and Raspberry Brie Crescents.

5. Garnish with fresh thyme and serve.

RASPBERRY BRIE CRESCENTS

*Preheat the oven to 375° and grease a mini muffin tin with cooking spray. On a lightly floured surface, unroll 1 **(8 oz.) tube crescent roll dough** and pinch together the seams. Cut into 24 rectangles. Press the rectangles into the muffin tin. Cut 1 (8 oz.) wheel of **Brie cheese** into small pieces and place 1 piece inside each dough-lined muffin tin. Top the Brie with a dollop of **raspberry preserves** and a pinch of **dried thyme**. Bake for 15 minutes or until the crescent dough is golden brown and the cheese is melted. **Makes 24***

Raspberry Brie Crescents

Whipped Honey-Ricotta

BERRIES *Galore*

Cheese: Whipped Honey-Ricotta *(recipe below)*, sharp white cheddar, blueberry cheddar

Bread & Crackers: cinnamon-raisin bread

Accompaniments: blueberries, blackberries, raspberries, strawberries, walnuts, golden raisins

Condiments & Dips: cherry preserves

Garnish: mint

1. Put the Whipped Honey-Ricotta, blueberries, blackberries, and cherry preserves in small bowls and place them on the board.

2. Arrange the sharp white cheddar and blueberry cheddar on the board.

3. Cut each slice of cinnamon raisin bread into quarters and place on the board.

4. Fill in any remaining gaps on the board with raspberries, strawberries, walnuts, and golden raisins.

5. Garnish with fresh mint and serve.

WHIPPED HONEY-RICOTTA

Blend 2 C. ricotta cheese, 4 oz. cream cheese, 1 T. sugar, ¼ C. honey, ¼ tsp. vanilla extract, and the juice of ½ lemon in a food processor until smooth. Transfer to a bowl and refrigerate until ready to serve. Drizzle with extra honey before serving.
Makes 2½ cups

All-AMERICAN Board

Cheeses: Pepper Jack, cheese curds, Maytag blue cheese

Charcuterie: mesquite-smoked turkey, summer sausage, Black Forest ham

Bread & Crackers: woven wheat crackers

Accompaniments: Overnight Bread & Butter Pickles *(recipe below)*, raspberries, pecans, almonds, dried cranberries, honey roasted peanuts

Condiments & Dips: raspberry preserves, honey mustard

Garnish: parsley

1. Put the Overnight Bread & Butter Pickles, raspberry preserves, and honey mustard in small bowls and place them on the board.

2. Arrange the Pepper Jack, cheese curds, Maytag blue cheese, mesquite-smoked turkey, summer sausage, and Black Forest ham on the board.

3. Nestle in a pile of woven wheat crackers.

4. Fill in any remaining gaps with raspberries, pecans, almonds, dried cranberries, and honey roasted peanuts.

5. Garnish with fresh parsley and serve.

OVERNIGHT BREAD & BUTTER PICKLES

*Thinly slice 4 **mini cucumbers** and place in a bowl. Toss with 3 T. **kosher salt** and chill in the refrigerator for 1 hour. Remove from the fridge and rinse with cold water. Drain and place the cucumbers in a pint jar. Combine ½ C. **sugar**, ¼ C. **brown sugar**, 1 C. **apple cider vinegar**, and 2 tsp. **mustard seed** in a saucepan over medium heat. Simmer until the sugar is dissolved. Remove from the heat and pour over the cucumbers. Let cool at room temperature for 30 minutes then seal and chill in the refrigerator overnight before serving. Store in the refrigerator for up to 3 weeks. **Makes 1 pint***

Overnight Bread & Butter Pickles

Herb & Garlic Dip

VEGGIE *lover's*

Cheese: feta, sharp cheddar, Havarti

Bread & Crackers: crackers

Accompaniments: Castelvetrano olives, marinated artichoke hearts, red grapes, cherry tomatoes, arugula, almonds, baby carrots, broccoli florets, sweet mini bells, radishes

Condiments & Dips: Herb & Garlic Dip *(recipe below)*, hummus

Garnish: dill

(1) Put the Castelvetrano olives, artichoke hearts, Herb & Garlic Dip, and hummus in small bowls and place them on the board.

(2) Arrange the feta, sharp cheddar, and Havarti on the board.

(3) Nestle in a stack or two of crackers.

(4) Fill in any remaining gaps with red grapes, cherry tomatoes, arugula, almonds, baby carrots, broccoli florets, sweet mini bells, and radishes.

(5) Garnish with fresh dill and serve.

HERB & GARLIC DIP

*In a mixing bowl, combine 1 C. **mayonnaise**, ½ C. **sour cream**, 1 T. **dried parsley**, 1 T. **dried chives**, ½ tsp. **dried tarragon**, 1 tsp. **dried dill**, 1 tsp. **minced garlic**, ½ tsp. **onion flakes**, ¼ tsp. **paprika**, ¼ tsp. **salt**, and ¼ tsp. **black pepper**. Refrigerate for several hours before serving to allow the flavors to develop. **Makes 1½ cups***

Breakfast of
CHAMPIONS

Cheese: garden vegetable cream cheese, Gouda, extra sharp white cheddar

Charcuterie: bacon, sausage patties

Bread & Crackers: bagel chips, pumpernickel bread, rye bread

Accompaniments: Honeycrisp apples, hard-cooked eggs, strawberries, sweet mini bells, blueberries

Condiments & Dips: Garlic-Chive Butter *(recipe below)*, apple butter

Garnish: dill, chives

1. Put the garden vegetable cream cheese, Garlic-Chive Butter, and apple butter in small bowls and place them on the board.

2. Arrange the Gouda, extra sharp white cheddar, bacon, and sausage on the board.

3. Nestle in some bagel chips, sliced pumpernickel, and sliced rye.

4. Fill in any remaining gaps with Honeycrisp apples, hard-cooked eggs, strawberries, sweet mini bells, and blueberries.

5. Garnish with fresh dill and chives.

GARLIC-CHIVE BUTTER

*Combine ½ C. softened **butter**, 1 tsp. **minced garlic**, 1 T. **chopped fresh chives**, ½ tsp. **dried parsley**, and ¼ tsp. **black pepper** in a bowl. Whisk until fully combined. Let rest for at least 1 hour to allow the flavors to meld. **Makes ½ cup***

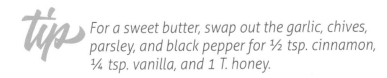

tip *For a sweet butter, swap out the garlic, chives, parsley, and black pepper for ½ tsp. cinnamon, ¼ tsp. vanilla, and 1 T. honey.*

Garlic-Chive Butter

Feta & Tomato Dip

1½ C. diced Roma tomatoes
¼ C. finely chopped green onion
8 oz. crumbled feta
¼ C. sliced Kalamata olives
¼ tsp. minced garlic
¼ tsp. black pepper

¼ tsp. dried dill
¼ tsp. dried marjoram
Olive oil
Balsamic vinegar
Fresh basil

① In a large mixing bowl, gently toss together the tomatoes, green onion, feta, olives, garlic, black pepper, dill, and marjoram. Cover and refrigerate for at least an hour before serving to allow the flavors to develop.

② Before serving, spread the dip on a small plate or dish. Finish with a light drizzle of olive oil and balsamic vinegar. Garnish with fresh basil. **Serve with crackers, flatbread, or pita chips.**

Included on the Summer Bounty board on page 66.

Bacon & Pepper Almond Brittle

serves 8

6 bacon strips
1 C. brown sugar
¼ C. butter
2 tsp. salt
½ tsp. coarse-ground black pepper
1½ C. unsalted almonds

1. Preheat the oven to 350° and grease a rimmed baking sheet with cooking spray.

2. Cook the bacon until crisp; drain and set aside to cool. Once cooled, crumble into small pieces.

3. In a small saucepan over medium heat, combine the brown sugar, butter, salt, and coarse-ground black pepper; stir until the sugar is dissolved and the mixture begins to bubble.

4. Add the almonds and the crumbled bacon to the saucepan; stir until coated and spread on the greased baking sheet. Bake 16 to 18 minutes.

5. Remove from the oven and allow to cool before breaking the brittle apart into bite-sized pieces. *Store in an airtight container in the refrigerator for up to 2 weeks.*

Included on the Spice it Up board on page 10.

23

Corn Salsa

MEXICAN *Fiesta*

Cheeses: Manchego, Cotija

Charcuterie: cured chorizo, honey ham

Bread & Crackers: corn tortillas, blue corn tortilla chips

Accompaniments: pickled jalapeños, pistachios, dried mango, avocados, radishes, sweet mini bells

Condiments & Dips: Corn Salsa *(recipe below)*

Garnish: cilantro, lime wedges

① Put the pickled jalapeños, pistachios, and Corn Salsa in small bowls and place them on the board.

② Arrange the Manchego, Cotija, chorizo, and honey ham on the board.

③ Slice the corn tortillas in half and place them on the board along with some blue corn tortilla chips.

④ Fill in any remaining gaps with dried mango, sliced avocado, radishes, and sweet mini bells.

⑤ Garnish with cilantro and lime wedges.

 *tip* *Sprinkle the sliced avocado with lime juice to keep it from turning brown.*

CORN SALSA

*Combine 1 (12 oz.) **bag corn** (thawed & drained), 2 seeded and chopped **jalapeños**, ½ C. finely chopped **red onion**, ½ C. chopped **cilantro**, 1 clove minced **garlic**, ½ tsp. salt, ½ tsp. **black pepper**, and the juice of 2 **limes**. **Makes 2 cups***

Perfect
PICKLES *Board*

Cheese: aged cheddar, Maytag blue cheese

Charcuterie: deli roast beef, summer sausage

Bread & Crackers: crackers, French bread

Accompaniments: dill pickle medley, Easy Pickled Asparagus *(recipe below)*, pickled beets, cocktail onions, almonds, sweet gherkins, dried apricots

Condiments & Dips: spicy brown mustard, raspberry preserves

Garnish: dill

① Put the dill pickle medley, Easy Pickled Asparagus, beets, cocktail onions, spicy brown mustard, and raspberry preserves in dishes and place them on the board.

② Arrange the aged cheddar, Maytag blue cheese, roast beef, and summer sausage on the board.

③ Add some crackers and sliced French bread.

④ Fill in any remaining gaps with almonds, sweet gherkins, and dried apricots.

⑤ Garnish with fresh dill and serve.

EASY PICKLED ASPARAGUS

*Wash and trim the ends off 2 lbs. **asparagus**. Boil a pot of water and prepare a bowl of ice water. Once the water reaches a boil, drop the asparagus in for 10 seconds. Drain the asparagus and transfer to the ice water.*

*Bring 1½ C. water, 1 C. **apple cider vinegar**, 1½ T. **salt**, and 1 T. **brown sugar** to a boil; remove from the heat and let cool. Meanwhile, place 4 **cloves garlic**, 3 **fresh dill sprigs**, 1 tsp. **mustard seed**, ½ tsp. **black peppercorns**, and ¼ tsp. **crushed red pepper** into the bottom of a quart jar. Fill with asparagus and top with brine. Seal and place in the refrigerator for at least 2 days before serving. Refrigerate up to 1 month. **Makes 1 quart**

Easy Pickled Asparagus

27

Maple Granola

YOGURT *Parfaits*

Base: vanilla yogurt, strawberry yogurt

Accompaniments: Maple Granola (recipe below), strawberries, blueberries, raspberries, kiwis, bananas, pecans, pepitas, chocolate-covered raisins

Garnish: mint

1. Put the yogurt and the Maple Granola in bowls and place them on the board.

2. Fill in any remaining gaps with strawberries, blueberries, raspberries, kiwis, bananas, pecans, pepitas, and chocolate-covered raisins.

3. Garnish with fresh mint and serve.

tip *Set out bowls and spoons and let guests build their own customized parfaits!*

MAPLE GRANOLA

*Preheat the oven to 300°. In a large mixing bowl, combine 2 C. **old-fashioned oats**, ½ C. **chopped pecans**, ¼ C. **sunflower seeds**, ¼ C. **maple syrup**, 3 T. **olive oil**, ½ tsp. **vanilla extract**, and ¼ tsp. **salt**. Spread the mixture in a thin layer on a baking sheet lined with parchment paper. Bake for 25 minutes. Cool before storing or serving. Store in an airtight container for up to 2 weeks. **Makes 2½ cups***

MEAT *lover's*

Cheese: Gouda

Charcuterie: pepperoni, mortadella, Genoa salami, soppressata salami, peppered salami, beef sticks, prosciutto

Bread & Crackers: crackers, Parmesan-Cheddar Crisps *(recipe below)*

Condiments & Dips: Refrigerator Pepper Jam *(recipe pg. 44)*, stone-ground mustard

Garnish: parsley

① Put the Refrigerator Pepper Jam and stone-ground mustard in small bowls and place them on the board.

② Arrange the Gouda, pepperoni, mortadella, Genoa salami, soppressata salami, peppered salami, beef sticks, and prosciutto on the board.

③ Nestle in a stack of crackers and some Parmesan-Cheddar Crisps.

④ Garnish with parsley and serve.

PARMESAN-CHEDDAR CRISPS

*Heat the oven to 350° and line a baking sheet with parchment paper. In a mixing bowl, combine ½ C. **grated Parmesan** and ½ C. **grated cheddar**. Spread about 1 T. of the cheese in a thin circle on the parchment paper; repeat with the remaining cheese. Bake 12 to 15 minutes or until the cheese is golden brown. Cool on the baking sheet before serving. Store in an airtight container for up to 1 week. **Makes about 18 crisps***

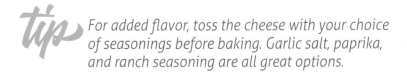 *For added flavor, toss the cheese with your choice of seasonings before baking. Garlic salt, paprika, and ranch seasoning are all great options.*

Parmesan-Cheddar Crisps →

31

Tomato & Goat Cheese Dip

SPANISH *tapas*

Cheeses: Manchego, Mahón

Charcuterie: cured chorizo, prosciutto

Bread & Crackers: French bread

Accompaniments: Spanish queen olives, almonds, green grapes, dried figs, pine nuts

Condiments & Dips: Tomato & Goat Cheese Dip

Garnish: parsley

1. Put the Spanish queen olives in a small bowl and place them on the board. Place the Tomato & Goat Cheese Dip beside the board.

2. Arrange the Manchego, Mahón, cured chorizo, and prosciutto on the board.

3. Slice a loaf of French bread; cut each slice into quarters and place them on the board.

4. Fill in any remaining gaps with almonds, green grapes, dried figs, and pine nuts.

5. Garnish with parsley and serve.

TOMATO & GOAT CHEESE DIP

*Preheat the broiler. In a small bowl, combine 1 C. **canned fire-roasted tomatoes**, 3 **cloves minced garlic**, 1 tsp. **sugar**, ½ tsp. **crushed red pepper**, ½ tsp. **black pepper**, ¼ tsp. **salt**, and ½ tsp. **paprika**. Transfer to an oven-safe dish.*

*Slice 4 oz. **fresh goat cheese** and dollop over the top of the sauce. Place under the broiler and cook for about 5 minutes or until the cheese bubbles. Garnish with **fresh parsley**.*
Serves 4

Homemade Cheese Crackers

2 T. softened butter
¾ C. shredded sharp cheddar cheese
½ C. shredded Parmesan cheese
¼ tsp. paprika
¼ tsp. garlic salt
½ C. flour
3 T. water

1. Preheat the oven to 375° and line a baking sheet with parchment paper.

2. In a mixing bowl, combine the butter, sharp cheddar cheese, Parmesan cheese, paprika, and garlic salt. Add the flour and water; stir until a dough forms.

3. Transfer the dough to a floured work surface and roll until it is about ⅛" thick. Use a pizza cutter to cut the dough into roughly 1" by 1" squares. Use a fork to poke a few holes into each cracker.

4. Arrange the crackers on the baking sheet and bake for 15 minutes or until golden brown. Let cool before transferring to an airtight container.

Included on the Autumn Harvest board on page 68.

Marinated Antipasto Skewers

1 (9 oz.) pkg. tortellini
1 (8 oz.) pkg. mozzarella pearls
1 C. Italian dressing
½ tsp. black pepper
¼ tsp. Italian seasoning

1 tsp. dried parsley
40 Kalamata olives
40 spinach leaves
40 pepperoni slices

1. Cook the tortellini according to package directions; drain and rinse.

2. Add the tortellini to a mixing bowl along with the mozzarella pearls, Italian dressing, black pepper, Italian seasoning, and dried parsley. Gently stir to combine, cover, and refrigerate for at least 2 hours, stirring halfway through.

3. To assemble, thread one tortellini, mozzarella pearl, olive, spinach leaf, and pepperoni slice onto a small wooden skewer, folding the pepperoni and spinach leaves in quarters before skewering.

Included on the Antipasto board on page 36.

ANTIPASTO

Cheese: Parmigiano-Reggiano, fresh mozzarella

Charcuterie: mortadella, capicola, soppressata salami

Bread & Crackers: cubed French bread

Accompaniments: marinated olives, marinated artichoke hearts, pepperoncini peppers, grape tomatoes, almonds, Marinated Antipasto Skewers *(recipe pg. 35)*

Dips & Condiments: Garlic Dipping Oil *(recipe below)*

Garnish: basil

1. Put the olives, artichoke hearts, pepperoncini peppers, and Garlic Dipping Oil in small bowls and place them on the board.

2. Arrange the Parmigiano-Reggiano, mozzarella, mortadella, capicola, and soppressata salami on the board.

3. Add a few piles of cubed French bread.

4. Fill in any remaining gaps with grape tomatoes, almonds, and Marinated Antipasto Skewers.

5. Garnish with fresh basil and serve.

GARLIC DIPPING OIL

*Pour 1 C. **extra virgin olive oil** into a small pan and set over medium-low heat. Add 1 **clove minced garlic** and heat until just warmed. Pour the olive oil into a shallow bowl. Immediately add ¼ C. **balsamic vinegar**, ¼ tsp. **salt**, and **black pepper** to taste. **Makes 1½ cups***

Garlic Dipping Oil

Hazelnut-Mascarpone
Spread

CHOCOLATE *galore*

Cheese: Brie

Bread & Crackers: sliced baguette

Accompaniments: chocolate-covered raisins, raspberries, blueberries, green grapes, almonds, roasted peanuts, dark chocolate

Condiments & Dips: Hazelnut-Mascarpone Spread *(recipe below)*, honey

Garnish: mint

1. Put the Hazelnut-Mascarpone Spread and honey in bowls and place them around the board.

2. Place the Brie on the board.

3. Add a few slices of baguette.

4. Fill in any remaining gaps with chocolate-covered raisins, raspberries, blueberries, green grapes, almonds, roasted peanuts, and dark chocolate.

5. Garnish with fresh mint and serve.

 *tips* *Cheddar and Monterey Jack also pair surprisingly well with chocolate.*

HAZELNUT-MASCARPONE SPREAD

*In a large mixing bowl, combine 1 C. **chocolate-hazelnut spread**, 1 C. **mascarpone**, ½ C. **softened cream cheese**, and a pinch of **sea salt** with a hand mixer. Transfer to a serving dish and top with chopped **hazelnuts** and **sea salt**. **Makes 2½ cups***

SWEET BRIE

Cheese: Honey-Almond Baked Brie *(recipe below)*

Charcuterie: prosciutto, Genoa salami

Bread & Crackers: toasted baguette slices

Accompaniments: golden raisins, pistachios, red grapes, Honeycrisp apples

Condiments & Dips: peach preserves

Garnish: rosemary

1. Put the golden raisins, pistachios, and peach preserves in bowls and place them around the board.

2. Arrange the prosciutto and Genoa salami on the board.

3. Add a few stacks of toasted baguette slices.

4. Fill in any remaining gaps with red grapes and sliced Honeycrisp apple.

5. Garnish with fresh rosemary.

6. Place the baked Brie beside the board and serve.

HONEY-ALMOND BAKED BRIE

*Preheat oven to 350°. Use a knife to trim the thin white rind off the top of an 8 oz. wheel of **Brie cheese**. Place the Brie in an oven-safe ramekin or skillet. Bake for 11 to 13 minutes or until softened. While the Brie bakes, combine ¼ C. **honey** and a **sprig of rosemary** in a small saucepan over low heat. Once warmed, stir in ½ C. **chopped roasted almonds**. Spoon the honey mixture over the Brie and garnish with a sprig of rosemary. **Serves 6***

 *The cheese loses its "gooeyness" relatively fast, so try to time it to come out of the oven right as guests arrive.*

Honey-Almond
Baked Brie

41

Basil Bruschetta

BRUSCHETTA *Board*

Cheese: fresh mozzarella, aged Asiago

Charcuterie: Genoa salami

Bread & Crackers: toasted baguette slices

Accompaniments: Kalamata olives, green grapes, grape tomatoes, almonds

Condiments & Dips: Basil Bruschetta *(recipe below)*, honey

Garnish: basil

1. Put the Kalamata olives, Basil Bruschetta, and honey in bowls and place them around the board.

2. Arrange the mozzarella, Asiago, and Genoa salami on the board.

3. Add a few stacks of toasted baguette, or fill a bread bowl and place it next to the board.

4. Fill in any remaining gaps with green grapes, grape tomatoes, and almonds.

5. Garnish with fresh basil and serve.

BASIL BRUSCHETTA

*In a medium bowl, combine 2½ C. chopped **tomatoes**, 2 minced **garlic cloves**, 2 T. **olive oil**, 1 T. **balsamic vinegar**, 1 tsp. **honey**, and 8 finely chopped **basil leaves**. Season to taste with **salt** and **pepper**. **Makes 2½ cups***

*Preheat oven to 350°. Slice a **baguette** loaf into ½" slices. Brush each slice with **olive oil** and sprinkle with **salt**. Bake for 10 minutes or until slightly golden.*

 Basil Bruschetta can be made up to 1 day ahead of time.

Refrigerator Pepper Jam

1 red bell pepper, finely chopped

1 yellow bell pepper, finely chopped

1 orange bell pepper, finely chopped

2 jalapeños, seeds removed and finely chopped

1 (1.75 oz.) pkg. fruit pectin

¾ C. distilled white vinegar

4 C. sugar

① Put the peppers, fruit pectin, and distilled white vinegar in a saucepan over medium heat. Bring the mixture to a full boil for 5 minutes, stirring frequently.

② Add the sugar and bring the mixture back to a boil; let boil for 2 minutes.

③ Remove the pan from the heat and pour the jam into containers. Allow to cool, uncovered, for 30 minutes. Seal and place in the refrigerator to allow the jam to set. Refrigerate in an airtight container for up to 1 month. Pair with cream cheese for a classic appetizer.

Included on the Meat Lover's board on page 30.

Rosemary Sea Salt Crackers

makes 40

1½ C. flour, plus more for dusting
1 tsp. sea salt, plus more for sprinkling
1 tsp. sugar
1 T. dried rosemary
3 T. olive oil, plus more for brushing
½ C. water

(1) Preheat oven to 475° and line a baking sheet with parchment paper.

(2) Whisk together the 1½ C. flour, 1 tsp. sea salt, sugar, and dried rosemary. Add 3 T. olive oil and the water; stir until fully combined.

(3) Turn the dough out onto a lightly floured surface. Roll out until it is about ⅛" thick, adding flour as needed to keep the dough from sticking to the rolling pin. Trim the thin edges of the dough to keep them from burning. Cut into roughly 2"x1" rectangles with a pizza cutter. Brush with olive oil and sprinkle with a pinch of sea salt.

(4) Arrange crackers in a single layer on the baking sheet. Bake for 13 to 17 minutes or until golden brown. Store in an airtight container at room temperature for up to 1 week.

Included on the Holiday Bliss board on page 70.

Bagel BRUNCH

Cheese: cream cheese, Garlic & Herb Boursin, Brie

Charcuterie: Nova lox, prosciutto

Bread & Crackers: plain bagels, everything bagels

Accompaniments: Pickled Red Onions *(recipe below)*, green onions, capers, avocados, cucumbers, raspberries, blueberries, arugula

Condiments & Dips: raspberry jam

Garnish: dill

1. Put the cream cheese, Pickled Red Onions, green onions, capers, and raspberry jam in bowls and place them on the board.

2. Arrange the Boursin, Brie, lox, and prosciutto on the board.

3. Cut the bagels into quarters and stack them on the board.

4. Fill in any remaining gaps with sliced avocado, sliced cucumber, raspberries, blueberries, and arugula.

5. Garnish with fresh dill and serve.

PICKLED RED ONIONS

*Slice 1 **red onion** as thin as you can. Place the slices inside a jar. In a measuring cup, combine ½ C. **apple cider vinegar**, 1 T. **sugar**, 1½ tsp. **salt**, and 1 C. **hot water**. Pour the pickling mixture over the sliced onions and let them sit for an hour at room temperature. Cover and chill in the refrigerator for at least 2 hours before serving. Store in the refrigerator for up to 3 weeks. **Makes about 1 pint***

Pickled red onions are versatile in the kitchen – use them to add a burst of flavor to tacos, hamburgers, hot dogs, and more.

Pickled Red Onions

47

Pimento Cheese

SOUTHERN BELL

Cheese: Pimento Cheese *(recipe below)*, sharp cheddar, Muenster

Charcuterie: Black Forest ham, browned andouille sausage

Bread & Crackers: crackers, pretzel chips

Accompaniments: dill pickle spears, pecans, roasted peanuts, peaches, strawberries, grape tomatoes

Condiments & Dips: orange marmalade

Garnish: parsley

1. Put the Pimento Cheese, pickles, and orange marmalade in bowls and place them around the board.

2. Arrange the sharp cheddar, Muenster, Black Forest ham, and andouille sausage on the board.

3. Nestle in a few stacks of crackers and pretzel chips.

4. Fill in any remaining gaps with pecans, roasted peanuts, peaches, strawberries, and grape tomatoes.

5. Garnish with fresh parsley and serve.

PIMENTO CHEESE

*Combine 2 C. grated **sharp cheddar cheese**, 8 oz. softened **cream cheese**, ½ C. **mayonnaise**, 4 oz. chopped **pimentos** (drained), ½ tsp. **garlic powder**, ½ tsp. **dried onion flakes**, ¼ tsp. **paprika**, ¼ tsp. **salt**, and ¼ tsp. **black pepper** with an electric mixer. Place in an airtight container and refrigerate for at least 2 hours to allow the flavors to develop.*
Serves 8

Customized
CROSTINI

Cheese: Garlic & Herb Boursin, blue cheese, Havarti

Charcuterie: prosciutto, Genoa salami

Bread & Crackers: toasted baguette slices

Accompaniments: marinated olives, arugula, almonds, golden raisins

Condiments & Dips: Strawberry Bruschetta *(recipe below)*, Caramelized Onion Jam *(recipe pg. 57)*, fig jam

Garnish: basil

1. Put the olives, Strawberry Bruschetta, Caramelized Onion Jam, and fig jam in bowls and place them on the board.

2. Arrange the Garlic & Herb Boursin, blue cheese, Havarti, prosciutto, and Genoa salami on the board.

3. Add some toasted baguette slices to the board.

4. Fill in any remaining gaps with arugula, almonds, and golden raisins.

5. Garnish with fresh basil and serve.

STRAWBERRY BRUSCHETTA

*In a large mixing bowl, combine 2 C. diced **fresh strawberries**, ½ C. finely sliced **basil leaves**, 2 T. **balsamic vinegar**, ½ T. **olive oil**, 1 tsp. **black pepper**, and ¼ tsp. **salt**. Cover and let sit for a couple hours to let the flavors develop before serving. **Makes 2½ cups***

Strawberry Bruschetta

Bacon-Wrapped
Stuffed Apricots

Hint of
SMOKE *Board*

Cheese: smoked black pepper Gouda, smoked cheddar

Charcuterie: smoked beef sticks, grilled smoked kielbasa, mesquite-smoked turkey

Bread & Crackers: toasted baguette slices, butter crackers

Accompaniments: dill pickles, Bacon-Wrapped Stuffed Apricots *(recipe below)*, almonds, pistachios, raspberries

Condiments & Dips: cherry preserves

Garnish: sage

1. Put the beef sticks, pickles, and cherry preserves in bowls and place them on the board.

2. Arrange the smoked Gouda, smoked cheddar, smoked kielbasa, and smoked turkey on the board.

3. Nestle some toasted baguette slices and butter crackers on the board.

4. Fill in any remaining gaps with Bacon-Wrapped Stuffed Apricots, almonds, pistachios, and raspberries.

5. Garnish with fresh sage and serve.

BACON-WRAPPED STUFFED APRICOTS

*Preheat oven to 400°. In a skillet, partially cook 18 **bacon strips** over medium heat for 6 minutes or until just brown but not crisp. Drain on paper towels and cut each strip in half.*

*Reserve 2 T. drippings in the skillet. Cook ½ C. **chopped walnuts** in the drippings over medium heat, stirring frequently, until lightly toasted. Add the walnuts, ¾ C. crumbled **blue cheese**, and ½ tsp. **dried sage** to a bowl; mix well. Transfer the mixture into a zippered plastic bag and cut the corner off to create a piping bag. Cut a small slit in 36 dried apricots; fill each **apricot** with the blue cheese mixture. Wrap 1 piece of bacon around each apricot and secure with a toothpick. Place on a rimmed baking sheet. Bake for 10 minutes. Serve warm. **Makes 36***

FRUIT *lover's*

Cheese: Brie, sharp cheddar, white cheddar

Bread & Crackers: toasted cinnamon-raisin bread, woven wheat crackers

Accompaniments: Honeycrisp apples, pears, kiwis, strawberries, mandarin oranges, almonds, dark chocolate, vanilla wafers, red grapes

Condiments & Dips: Delectable Fruit Dip, honey

① Put the Delectable Fruit Dip and honey in bowls and place them on the board.

② Arrange the Brie, sharp cheddar, and white cheddar on the board.

③ Add some cinnamon-raisin bread and woven wheat crackers.

④ Fill in any remaining gaps with sliced Honeycrisp apple, sliced pear, sliced kiwi, strawberries, sliced mandarin oranges, almonds, dark chocolate, vanilla wafers, and red grapes.

 *Gouda, goat cheese, and fresh mozzarella also pair well with fruit.*

DELECTABLE FRUIT DIP

*Add 8 oz. softened **cream cheese** to a mixing bowl and beat on low speed until smooth. Slowly add 1 C. **plain yogurt** and continue to mix until combined. Add ½ C. **brown sugar**, ¼ tsp. **cinnamon**, and 1 tsp. **vanilla extract**; mix until combined. Cover and place in the refrigerator for at least 1 hour before serving. **Makes 1½ cups***

Delectable Fruit Dip

Spinach Cheese Puffs

½ C. cream cheese
½ C. shredded mozzarella
¼ C. ricotta cheese
¼ C. finely chopped spinach leaves
1 clove minced garlic
1 tsp. dried parsley
1 tsp. chopped chives
¼ tsp. salt
¼ tsp. black pepper
1 (14 oz.) pkg. puff pastry, thawed
Flour for dusting
1 egg

1. In a mixing bowl, combine cream cheese, mozzarella, ricotta, spinach, garlic, parsley, chives, salt, and black pepper.

2. Unfold the pastry sheets on a floured work surface. Cut each sheet into 12 rectangles *(24 total)*. Add about 1 teaspoon of filling to each.

3. Whisk together the egg. Brush the edges of each pastry square with egg wash and fold in half. Press the edges with a fork to seal. Place them in the refrigerator to chill for 15 minutes.

4. Preheat the oven to 400°. Bake for 20 to 22 minutes or until golden and puffy.

Included on the Spring Greens board on page 64.

Caramelized Onion Jam

3 T. olive oil
3 white onions, thinly sliced
2 tsp. minced garlic
2 T. whole grain mustard
¼ C. brown sugar
2 T. honey

¼ C. balsamic vinegar
2 C. beef broth
¼ tsp. dried thyme
¼ tsp. black pepper
¼ tsp. salt

① Pour the olive oil into the bottom of a heavy pot over medium heat. Add the onions and garlic; cook uncovered for ten minutes, stirring every few minutes.

② Add the mustard, brown sugar, honey, balsamic vinegar, broth, thyme, black pepper, and salt; stir to combine. Cover the pot, lower the heat slightly, and let the mixture simmer for 30 minutes.

③ Uncover the pot, stir, and cook until most of the liquid is gone and the onions reach a jam-like consistency, approximately 50 minutes.

Included on the Customized Crostini board on page 50.

57

German Raspberry Mustard

Classic
GERMAN

Cheese: Gouda, caraway cheddar

Charcuterie: Braunschweiger, summer sausage, grilled bratwurst

Bread & Crackers: rye chips, pretzel chips, pretzel bread

Accompaniments: sweet gherkins, green grapes, hazelnuts

Condiments & Dips: German Raspberry Mustard *(recipe below)*

Garnish: parsley

① Put the sweet gherkins and German Raspberry Mustard in small bowls and place them on the board.

② Arrange the Gouda, caraway cheddar, Braunschweiger, summer sausage, and bratwurst on the board.

③ Nestle in some rye chips and pretzels chips. Slice a loaf of pretzel bread and place it next to the board.

④ Fill in any remaining gaps with green grapes and hazelnuts.

⑤ Garnish with fresh parsley and serve.

 *Braunschweiger can be served in slices or spread on crackers.*

GERMAN RASPBERRY MUSTARD

*In a small saucepan, mix 2 T. **brown sugar** and 1 T. **balsamic vinegar**; cook over medium heat until the sugar dissolves. Reduce the heat to low and add ½ pt. **fresh raspberries**; cook 10 minutes more. Add 1 T. **dry mustard**, 1 T. **mustard seeds**, ¼ tsp. **salt**, and ¼ tsp. **black pepper**; cook 10 minutes more. **Makes 1 cup***

MEDITERRANEAN

Cheese: feta, Manchego

Charcuterie: soppressata salami

Bread & Crackers: pita chips, flatbread

Accompaniments: marinated artichoke hearts, Kalamata olives, cucumbers, pistachios, grape tomatoes

Condiments & Dips: hummus, Tzatziki Dip *(recipe below)*

Garnish: dill

1. Put the artichoke hearts, olives, hummus, and Tzatziki Dip in small bowls and place them on the board.

2. Arrange the feta, Manchego, and salami on the board.

3. Nestle in some pita chips. Cut each flatbread into quarters and place them alongside the board.

4. Fill in any remaining gaps with cucumbers, pistachios, and grape tomatoes.

5. Garnish with fresh dill and serve.

TZATZIKI DIP

*Grate ½ large **cucumber** and squeeze out the excess moisture. Combine the grated cucumber, 1½ C. **plain full-fat Greek yogurt**, 1 clove **minced garlic**, 2 T. **extra virgin olive oil**, 1 T. **distilled white vinegar**, ½ tsp. **salt**, ¼ tsp. **black pepper**, and 1 T. **minced fresh dill** in a large bowl. Cover and refrigerate for at least 2 hours to allow the flavors to meld. Serve chilled. **Makes 2 cups***

Tzatziki Dip

Crispy Chickpeas

BUDGET *Board*

Cheese: Colby-Jack, Swiss

Charcuterie: Black Forest ham, pepperoni, beef sticks

Bread & Crackers: butter crackers

Accompaniments: sweet gherkins, Crispy Chickpeas *(recipe below)*, pears, dried cranberries, almonds, arugula

Condiments & Dips: peach preserves

1. Put the sweet gherkins, Crispy Chickpeas, and peach preserves in small bowls and place them on the board.

2. Arrange the Colby-Jack, Swiss, Black Forest ham, pepperoni, and beef sticks on the board.

3. Nestle in a stack of butter crackers.

4. Fill in any remaining gaps with sliced pears, dried cranberries, almonds, and arugula.

CRISPY CHICKPEAS

*Preheat the oven to 400°. Drain and rinse **2 (15 oz.) cans of chickpeas**. Let air-dry for a few minutes before patting dry with a paper towel. In a large mixing bowl, combine the chickpeas, 2 T. **olive oil**, 2 tsp. **salt**, and ¼ tsp. **garlic powder**. Spread in a single layer on a rimmed baking sheet. Roast for 50 minutes, turning halfway through. Toss the roasted chickpeas with ½ tsp. **parsley**, ¼ tsp. **black pepper**, and ¼ tsp. **paprika**. Serve while the chickpeas are slightly warm and crispy. **Makes 2 cups***

 *Reheat any leftover Crispy Chickpeas in a skillet over medium heat for 5 minutes, stirring often. This will crisp them up again.*

Spring GREENS *Board*

Cheese: blue cheese, Swiss, Brie

Charcuterie: soppressata salami, mortadella

Bread & Crackers: woven wheat crackers

Accompaniments: cocktail onions, sugar snap peas, mini cucumbers, macadamia nuts, Spinach Cheese Puffs *(recipe pg. 56)*

Condiments & Dips: Green Goddess Dip *(recipe below)*

Garnish: basil

1. Put the cocktail onions and Green Goddess Dip in small bowls and place them on the board.

2. Arrange the blue cheese, Swiss, Brie, soppressata salami, and mortadella on the board.

3. Fill a bowl with woven wheat crackers and place it alongside the board.

4. Fill in any remaining gaps with sugar snap peas, mini cucumbers, macadamia nuts, and Spinach Cheese Puffs.

5. Garnish with fresh basil and serve.

GREEN GODDESS DIP

*Combine 2 C. packed **arugula**, ½ C. **fresh basil leaves**, 3 T. **chopped fresh chives**, 1 T. **chopped fresh parsley**, and ½ tsp. **lemon zest** in a food processor; blend for 5 seconds. Add ½ C. **mayonnaise**, ¼ C. **sour cream**, 1 tsp. **Dijon mustard**, 2 **garlic cloves**, ¼ tsp. **salt**, and ¼ tsp. **black pepper**. Blend until all ingredients are finely chopped. Cover and chill until ready to serve. **Makes 1½ cups**

Green Goddess Dip

Prosciutto-Wrapped
Cantaloupe

Summer
BOUNTY *Board*

Cheese: aged cheddar, Camembert, Colby-Jack

Charcuterie: summer sausage, honey ham, mesquite-smoked turkey

Bread & Crackers: woven wheat crackers, whole-wheat crackers

Accompaniments: Prosciutto-Wrapped Cantaloupe *(recipe below)*, strawberries, peaches, grape tomatoes, mini cucumbers

Condiments & Dips: peach preserves, Feta & Tomato Dip *(recipe pg. 22)*, balsamic glaze *(recipe below)*

Garnish: basil

1. Put the peach preserves and Feta & Tomato Dip in bowls and place them around the board.

2. Arrange the aged cheddar, Camembert, Colby-Jack, summer sausage, honey ham, and smoked turkey on the board.

3. Nestle in a few stacks of woven wheat and whole-wheat crackers.

4. Fill in any remaining gaps with Prosciutto-Wrapped Cantaloupe, strawberries, sliced peaches, grape tomatoes, and mini cucumbers.

5. Garnish with fresh basil and serve.

PROSCIUTTO-WRAPPED CANTALOUPE

*Cut a **cantaloupe** into 1" squares. Cut a piece of **prosciutto** in half lengthwise and across so it's in four pieces. Wrap a piece of cantaloupe in prosciutto. Place a **basil leaf** on top and pierce with a toothpick to hold it together. Repeat for each skewer you want to make.*

*For the **balsamic glaze**, combine ½ C. **balsamic vinegar**, ¼ C. **honey**, and ¼ tsp. **garlic salt** in a small saucepan over medium heat. Cook and stir until the mixture begins to foam. Reduce heat to low and simmer, stirring occasionally, for 10 minutes. Drizzle over the skewers before serving.*

Autumn
HARVEST *Board*

Cheeses: aged cheddar, blue cheese

Charcuterie: Maple Candied Bacon *(recipe below)*

Bread & Crackers: sweet potato chips, Homemade Cheese Crackers *(recipe pg. 34)*

Accompaniments: pickled beets, pecans, pumpkin seeds, Granny Smith apples, pepitas

Condiments & Dips: maple syrup, spicy brown mustard

Garnish: sage

1. Put the beets, maple syrup, and spicy brown mustard in small bowls and place them on the board. Fill a bowl with sweet potato chips and place it alongside the board.

2. Arrange the aged cheddar, blue cheese, and Maple Candied Bacon on the board.

3. Nestle in a pile of Homemade Cheese Crackers.

4. Fill in any remaining gaps with pecans, pumpkin seeds, Granny Smith apple slices, and pepitas.

5. Garnish with fresh sage and serve.

 *Sprinkle the apples with lemon juice to keep them from turning brown after they've been cut.*

MAPLE CANDIED BACON

*Preheat the oven to 350°. In a small bowl, combine 2 T. **brown sugar**, ¼ C. **maple syrup**, and 1 T. **apple cider vinegar**. Set aside. Spread 1 lb. **bacon** on a large rimmed baking sheet. Bake for 12 minutes, turning halfway through. Remove the bacon from the oven and brush both sides generously with the brown sugar mixture. Return to the oven and bake 5 minutes more. Brush with the sugar mixture every 5 minutes until the bacon is caramelized and crisp, about 20 minutes. Remove from the oven and set on a rack to cool. **Serves 8**

Maple Candied Bacon

69

Cran-Orange Sauce

HOLIDAY *Bliss*

Cheeses: feta, Gruyère, cranberry-cinnamon cheddar

Charcuterie: peppered salami, mesquite-smoked turkey

Bread & Crackers: Rosemary Sea Salt Crackers *(recipe pg. 45)*

Accompaniments: Marcona almonds, mandarin oranges, hazelnuts, pomegranate seeds, green grapes, dried cranberries

Condiments & Dips: Cran-Orange Sauce *(recipe below)*

Garnish: rosemary

1. Put the Cran-Orange Sauce in a small bowl and place it on the board.

2. Arrange the feta, Gruyère, cranberry-cinnamon cheddar, peppered salami, and mesquite-smoked turkey on the board.

3. Nestle in a stack or two of Rosemary Sea Salt Crackers.

4. Fill in any remaining gaps with Marcona almonds, mandarin oranges, hazelnuts, pomegranate seeds, green grapes, and dried cranberries.

5. Garnish with fresh rosemary and serve.

 *Rosemary is the perfect winter-themed garnish because it remembles pine greenery.*

CRAN-ORANGE SAUCE

*Bring 1 C. **orange juice**, ½ C. **sugar**, and ¼ tsp. **salt** to a boil in a medium saucepan. Add 1 (12 oz.) bag of **fresh cranberries** and the **zest of ½ orange**; return to a boil. Reduce heat to low and simmer, uncovered, until the cranberries split and the sauce thickens. Cool to room temperature and serve. Garnish with **orange zest**. **Makes 2 cups***

Board Inspirations

Recipes